Celebrating the 100th Day of School

Katie Peters

GRL Consultant Diane Craig,
Certified Literacy Specialist

Lerner Publications ◆ Minneapolis

Note from a GRL Consultant
This Pull Ahead leveled book has been carefully designed for beginning readers. A team of guided reading literacy experts has reviewed and leveled the book to ensure readers pull ahead and experience success.

Lerner Publications
An imprint of Lerner Publishing Group, Inc.
241 First Avenue North
Minneapolis, MN 55401 USA

For reading levels and more information, look up this title at www.lernerbooks.com.

Main body text set in Memphis Pro 24/39
Typeface provided by Linotype.

Photo Acknowledgments
The images in this book are used with the permission of: © Zerbor/Shutterstock Images, p. 3; © anek.soowannaphoom/Shutterstock Images, pp. 4–5, 16 (right); © stockfour/Shutterstock Images, pp. 6–7, 16 (left); © Monkey Business Images/Shutterstock Images, pp. 8–9, 10–11; © Rawpixel.com/Shutterstock Images, pp. 12–13, 16 (middle); © Pond Saksit/Shutterstock Images, pp. 14–15.

Front Cover: © Brocreative/Adobe Stock

Library of Congress Cataloging-in-Publication Data

Names: Peters, Katie, author.
Title: Celebrating the 100th day of school / Written by Katie Peters.
Other titles: Celebrating the hundredth day of school
Description: Minneapolis, MN : Lerner Publications, [2026] | Series: Let's celebrate holidays (Pull ahead readers – nonfiction) | Includes index. | Audience: Ages 4–7 | Audience: Grades K–1 | Summary: "What do you do on the 100th day of school? Follow along with leveled text and engaging photographs to see what many classrooms do to celebrate. Pairs with the story, Our Class Counts to 100"—Provided by publisher.
Identifiers: LCCN 2024039749 (print) | LCCN 2024039750 (ebook) | ISBN 9798765668702 (library binding) | ISBN 9798765684375 (paperback) | ISBN 9798765678534 (epub)
Subjects: LCSH: Hundredth Day of School—Juvenile literature.
Classification: LCC LB3533 .P48 2026 (print) | LCC LB3533 (ebook) | DDC 370.2—dc23/eng/20240923

LC record available at https://lccn.loc.gov/2024039749
LC ebook record available at https://lccn.loc.gov/2024039750

Manufactured in the United States of America
1 – CG – 7/15/25

Table of Contents

Celebrating the 100th Day of School

We read on the 100th day.

We draw on the 100th day.

We write on the 100th day.

We count on the 100th day.

We play on the 100th day.